Crowdsourcing With Amazon Mechanical Turk

Robert Plank
&
Thom Lancaster

First published 2011, All Rights Reserved.

No part of this publication may be reproduced in any form or by any means, including scanning, photocopying, or otherwise without prior written permission of the copyright holder.

By reading this document, you assume all risks associated with using the advice given below, with a full understanding that you, solely, are responsible for anything that may occur as a result of putting this information into action in any way, and regardless of your interpretation of the advice.

Printed in the United States of America

The content for this book is sourced mainly from training seminars carried out by Robert Plank, and is used under license.

Dedicated to Internet Marketers everywhere, with thanks.

Crowdsourcing With Amazon Mechanical Turk

Table of Contents

About The Authors

Robert Plank is a 26 year old home-owner from California. He is a full time Internet Marketer and PHP programmer.

To find out more about Robert, visit RobertPlankTraining.com.

Thom Lancaster is a UK based Internet Marketer. He has a particular interest in product creation.

To find out more about Thom, visit ThomLancaster.com.

Foreward

Here's what Wikipedia has to say about Crowdsourcing:

> "Crowdsourcing is the act of outsourcing tasks, traditionally performed by an employee or contractor, to an undefined, large group of people or community (a "crowd"), through an open call."

One really excellent way to get started with Crowdsourcing, with a very limited budget, is to use the Amazon.com Mechanical Turk service.

RobertPlankTraining.com

Robert Plank is a master at picking up new technologies and services, and his insights into the Mechanical Turk, as shared in this book, are faultless.

I particularly like Robert's system for calculating how to much to charge to have jobs completed for you on Mechanical Turk. It removes all the guesswork and makes it easy to get started.

There are also some excellent case studies about using Mechanical Turk for Crowdsourcing, and I'd advise you to pay particular attention to these chapters.

RobertPlankTraining.com

Above all, do dive in and get started using Mechanical Turk for Crowdsourcing. It's what this great service is there for.

Thom Lancaster
ThomLancaster.com

Chaper 1 - Introduction

In this book, we are going to talk about how to make money using Amazon.com's Mechanical Turk Crowdsourcing Service.

First of all, we need to understand what crowdsourcing is.

I know that many of you have tried to do some freelancing and it's really easy to get carried away and make your project super big and make all kinds of plans for it and then give it to somebody to make and they charge you a huge fee and it never gets done.

So what do you do?

Well instead of getting them to write a whole book for you, you cut it up into pieces, maybe you give a third of the book to three different people and if one guy fails, so what. Or maybe you cut up the book into different chapters and if one guy fails, so what. Or maybe you cut up the chapters themselves into tiny little articles.

So the idea here with Crowdsourcing is that you cut it up into such little jobs that you only pay a few cents or maybe a dollar for someone to accomplish a really simple unskilled job.

You have lots of people perform lots and lots of 10 cent jobs or 25 cent jobs, instead of $50 to $100 ones. If you were doing forum posts and you'd paid someone say 50 cents per post to a forum, and you paid them $50 and say that for $50 you make 100 posts to my forum.

You're going to get a guy who registers maybe 10 different forum accounts and posts 10 posts at each account as creatively as he can and if he's not very good it's going to be pretty obvious that all those posts came from the same person.

The idea with Crowdsourcing that same job is you take those 50 cent forum jobs, maybe even 25 cent, and you give those jobs to 100 different people. So you end up paying $25 and a 100 people take those 25 cent jobs - what you end up having is a very diverse set of responses and questions on the forum.

So these are the kind of things that will work very well for you with the Turk especially if you word it the right way.

I'm going to get into this in a little bit but the thing you need to remember, and I'm going to repeat myself here, is that you can't use this kind of stuff to get people to click on ads or you can't use this kind of stuff as advertising but you can word it in such a way (like "I'm doing research") that would help you out if the quality control people were checking on your jobs.

So you could say: "I'm doing research and want to know what the top ten questions a layperson has about this topic? So because you're a layperson I want you to go to this forum, sign up using some random name then start a new thread and ask some question in this niche and then list maybe three or four sentences about it. To do the research you would look on this site, for example go to Google and type in this word, and find out what the common questions are."

Or you do this with a blog post. You say "Here is my blog post right here. I'll pay you 50 cents if you read the post and you type out a one paragraph response to this. So it could be a question or your thoughts or maybe this makes you think of something else" - but you make it very clear you are doing research so you don't want to word it in such a way that "oh I want you to fill out a bunch of blog comments", you just say "I'm doing research and want to know your personal opinion for something" because Amazon's idea behind making this service is they want to be able to mostly (not completely but mostly) automate tasks that cannot be performed by a computer.

Stuff like responding to blog posts or finding out the common pain points in a niche are not very well done by computers. The same thing with stuff like transcriptions – there's always going to be speech to text software, but it's never going to be 100% and humans are always going to beat computers as transcriptionists, at least in the near future.

So to start off the really simple Crowdsourcing techniques you can use are forum and blog posts to fill out your forums and blogs, and then you can even get into stuff like transcriptions, where you take an audio file and cut it up into several small pieces and have people listen to say 30 seconds or one minute of audio and transcribe that. But stuff like that is going to require a special script and some special coding because you want to give these different people a random section of the audio. Stuff like forum blog posts are what you can get started with right away.

Chapter 2 - Is The Turk Better Than Freelancing?

Yes and no. Like I said with the example with all the forum posts you have a hundred different people making a hundred different forum posts instead of one guy trying to make a hundred. So it's going to be a lot of fresh energy and it's going to be less repetition, so you're going to have all kinds of different personalities, different writing styles, people are going to write short or long sentences, some people might make more typos or less typos – it'll look more real and it'll be more organic.

You don't have to worry about making a huge project and having a huge amount of money on the line and people missing deadlines. If you make a job and you word it incorrectly and people don't finish the task or you charge too much or too little, no big deal you just cancel the job. In fact I have cancelled many Turk human intelligence tasks (Amazon's name for jobs), I've cancelled many jobs before they completed just because I wanted to open it back up again with a refined set of instructions, because you're always going to make little tweaks to your instructions - you're never going to explain stuff completely dummy-proof.

It's better than freelancing for those reasons, mostly the less repetition, but the thing you need to remember is that you're hiring unskilled labor. You cannot assume that your Crowd Source people are experts at anything. You can't assume that they can make a video for you. You can't assume that they are going to write a bunch of articles for you. If you can find people like that that's more skilled labor and you're going to need to pay them more at which point it becomes less of a hassle to go towards the traditional freelance route.

But just for the unskilled labor to fill out a bunch of forum posts or get people to rate stuff or get people to transcribe stuff, this is perfect.

Chapter 3 - Terminology

Here's the terminology you're going to need to know when making a Mechanical Turk job. Actually the most important term is going to be a 'HIT' – a Human Intelligence Task. Amazon.com just loves to invent new terminology as you knew if you watched my video about Amazon S3 where they like to say "oh instead of folders they are called buckets and instead of a username it's called an access identifier, instead of a password it's called a secret key." They have these things called jobs, which is really a Human Intelligence Task.

When you create a Human Intelligence Task you are going to need to know a few things. You are going to need to know is it single or multi-person? So is one person doing the job or are a group of people doing the job?

How long will these people have to complete the task? That doesn't mean how long they will take to complete the task, this means what is the maximum amount of time it can possibly take someone to complete this task because, if someone starts a job and they wait too long and the task expires, they can't finish it, it just expires and even if they did some of the work they cannot get credit for it.

How much are you going to pay people for this job? That is something that you're going to have to figure out on your own by looking at other Human Intelligence Tasks and by posting lots of small jobs and figuring out – is the quality good enough for the price you're paying? Is the response enough? Are enough people taking the job? You might have to move your price up or down depending on those factors.

You need a good enough job description because remember you are going to be dealing with people who have no skills, these are people who are willing to put in a few minutes time for pennies. These are people who don't necessarily know English as their first language. Personally my experience with the Turk is that I get a few people taking jobs during the day but at night when the other side of the world, the overseas world, wakes up, that's when the real jobs come in. So you're going to have to be very careful about how you word your jobs, you're going to have to make instructions very short, very hard to break and very easy to understand because your job takers will not necessarily be fluent in English.

Chapter 4 - Getting Started

Here's how you get started.

You start the job and you're going to have to sign up at the Turk Service and probably hand over a credit card so that they can automatically bill you. I think you put in a deposit first, when you start a job they make you pay the money in advance.

So if you make a job that's going to have 100 people at 50 cents each, that means you require $50 and they'll make you pay $50 plus an extra little fee for them to process it.

When you get started and you've got your credit card on file and your account created for the Amazon.com Mechanical Turk – you can just search for 'Mechanical Turk' - the URL is MTurk.Amazon.com, you create the job and you choose if you want to have a single or multi-person. To be honest, I have not messed around too much with the single person, I'm more of a multi-person guy because it's unskilled labor. If I want skilled single person labor I would go to one of the regular freelance sites or ask around and get a good recommendation for a good graphic designer, a copywriter or an article writer or something like that.

If you're going to do a single person job a typical job is to post a 5 minute MP3 file and pay $5 to get it transcribed, so that's an easy way to start.

You take maybe a transcript or an interview, an audio product where you are just speaking and explaining some topic, and chop out the first 5 minutes and post the first 5 minutes as a job and pay $5 to get it transcribed.

Guess what, if you have a 20 minute audio, all you need to do is cut up the audio into 4 parts (which will take you 30 seconds if you have experience with that), upload all 4 different files, create the instructions for the first part and then post the job - it's a $5 job. Edit it a tiny little bit to make it link to part 2 of the MP3 file and ask to get to transcribed, post that as a job - you just post that 4 times at $5 each and you've got a 20 minute MP3 file which is going to be about 20 pages transcribed for $20. However they might not take that job or it might be of low quality so you might have to adjust your price.

Another thing to try is post a video or an article, so this could be one of your articles on EzineArticles, it could be one of your YouTube videos, and pay $5 for a review. So you say "Watch this video, I don't want you to transcribe it, I just want you to watch it and write out the main points and basically explain the gist of what I'm saying in this video so that if someone read the text they would understand everything in the video and they would get the idea but it wouldn't be word for word".

This is a good way for you to just record a bunch of quick videos and then get people to rewrite those videos as articles.

This is something you can build in to your sites if you have a little bit of coding experience or if you have a programmer who can whip out a simple add-on to your site for $20.

Let say you ran an article directory and you had a URL where it would give somebody a random unapproved article and it would ask them to either approve it or deny it. Let's say you ran an article directory that gets a decent amount of spam submissions so you would create all these Turk jobs and you would say "I want you to go in, there are 10 random articles listed here, I'll give you $2 to do this. You just quickly go in and the articles that are really spam, delete those, and the ones that are real, add those."

Or if you ran a photo-sharing site like Flickr you could show images and ask if they are appropriate or not appropriate and just give them 20 or 30 at a time.

Or you could ask them to tag the images so you could say “If you see this picture and it’s a picture of a little boy flying a kite on a grassy hill and there are clouds in the background, what are the 5 words that come into mind when you first see this?”

He might say “clouds, kite, boy, hill, fun”, stuff like that.

So those are some ideas of how you would get started having a single person or a multi-person job.

Chapter 5 - The Sheep Market

Here is a cool story that maybe will inspire you about somebody who posted a multi-person Amazon.com Mechanical Turk job. This guy was an artist and he wanted to collect a bunch of hand-drawn pictures of sheep for an art project at a photo gallery - he ended up monetizing it as a website and a book. The idea was he needed 10,000 sheep to put on this poster, on this huge piece of artwork. So he listed the job and he said "Draw a sheep facing to the left and I will pay you 2 cents for this". He asked for 10,000 workers to do this.

He linked to a site where there was a Flash based drawing tool where you could use your mouse to draw a picture of a sheep. It would save it and give a confirmation number and then he would tell people to copy and paste that back into the Turk interface so that he could approve their entry and they would get credit for drawing this sheep.

So he did that 2 cents each, 10,000 sheep and if you do the math that means he spent $200 to get 10,000 sheep drawn. The average drawing time on each was a little over a minute and a half and that means the average wage paid to each person was 69 cents an hour.

You might think that's really low wages but consider the fact that these are mostly overseas people and that these are people who are just screwing around and doodling and they are probably going to waste that time anyway so why not make a few cents for that work?

He rejected 6% of the sheep, so some of the sheep were facing the wrong way or were blank or weren't sheep at all, I think some of the wrong-facing sheep actually made it into the final work. He rejected about 6% so a task as simple as 'draw a sheep facing to the left' was miss-done by 6%.

You might attribute that to the low wage or the low intelligence required to draw the sheep but that's something to consider if you get really bad submissions, maybe you need to bump up your wage. So if you're willing to let $500 go, maybe pay 5 cents each instead of 2 cents each.

The collection period was 40 days, so it's not like all these sheep came flowing in overnight. If you're impatient it might take you a while to get all this stuff. It took him 40 days to get the sheep; he got in 11 sheep per hour which is every 5 minutes he got a new hand-drawn sheep.

It's good to get work done by a lot of people but it's not necessarily superfast, it's not necessarily instant.

He drew a bunch of sheep, what did he do with it?

He created a website showing how each sheep was drawn, I forget the name of the website but if you just Google for 'Turk sheep' you can find it and he shows you every single sheep that was ever drawn. You click on one and you can see what steps they took to draw it, so you can see that for example, first they drew the head, then they drew the nose, then they drew the body. Or first they drew the feet, and then they drew the body. And you can see exactly the steps they took to draw that sheep and that was just because of the script or the software that he used on his site where people could draw these sheep right on the screen.

That part of it is up to you. The only job of the Turk is to get your workers onto your websites. So if you have this script that handles the transcriptions of audios, handles the transcriptions of videos, whatever, you'll need the special software to get that to work, which is why I recommended you begin by paying for simple blog posts or forum posts just to test it out, to see how you word stuff and how quickly you can expect the submissions to come in and figure out the quality of it all.

He made this website where you could click on any of these sheep and see how it was drawn. Then he published a print book containing all the sheep so you could buy this cute little book and it was a

$20 or $30 book, and you could flip through and every single page has a few hundred more sheep.

Then he made a huge poster and I think he might have made several posters, and he displayed it in an art gallery. He allows you to mail order specific sheep online, so if you find one of the sheep that you really like you can get a different size, like a poster size or a wallet size or a hanging on the wall size, so he's monetized this really well. He has a print book, he has the mail order, he made money from having it in the art gallery and he got tons of media coverage where, guess what, they promoted his website – they gave his name and his URL. They were talking about how weird this was that you get people from all over the internet drawing sheep for not very much money. Of course they played it up “oh it’s the teamwork and it’s all about the future”, but the bottom line was he paid people to do a job. But because of the internet he connected and got a lot more people to do a job that maybe, if he had tried to get people off the street, would have been a lot more work whereas with this project, he created the job, he said he needed 10,000 of these, waited a month and a half and at the end of the month and a half he had 10,000 sheep drawn for him.

So you might think at first that a project like that only has artsy value or that you can only use the Turk for testing purposes and that’s partly true. Like I said before, you cannot ask people to click on ads or provide personal info. So you can say "Make up a fake name", but I personally don't want them to make up a foreign sounding name, so I say "Go to this website, like FakeNameGenerator or choose an Americanized name and use that as your name if you need to use it on a blog post or something".

Set the time limit to 5 times to 10 times the actual time it should take them to complete it because remember you're dealing with people who maybe are multi-tasking because if you're only getting paid 69 cents an hour, you'll probably be doing something else that's more worth your time.

Some people like I said don't speak English as a first language so they might work a lot slower. I needed blog comments once and I think I asked for 10 minutes at a time. A lot of people would take the job and then read the blog post and start typing and the job would expire and they would get no credit for their work.

If you're doing something like a blog post, even one single blog post, set it to like half an hour or 60 minutes. You're not going to drive people away because it looks like a half an hour or a 60 minute job. You can even say in the description "This should only take you 5 minutes but just in case something comes up or you work slowly, I'm going to give you a 60 minute maximum time limit".

Explain it in very step-by-step instructions. So you say, go to this site, don't click on anything else, you click on this box, you type in the name from the fake name generator, you type in the email address 'noreply@example.com' because it's my blog and I control it and I'm not using it to spam, I'm just using it for testing purposes and I will know that anyone who posts as noreply@example.com is one of you testing people, one of my research assistants.

Then you write and I always like to ask if they have a word count or paragraph or sentence count because you just know that if you're paying someone a few cents they're going to try to half-ass it because we all do, there's nothing racist about it, we've all half-assed stuff in school, at work – if we can get away with the minimum amount of work possible we will. So if you tell somebody "I need 5 sentences" they will write all 5 sentences usually because they want to get paid for the work and they know that if they write 3 sentences when you asked for 5 you're probably not going to approve the job.

Those are my tips about using the Turk. Don't have them click ads, don't use it to provide personal information or build a list or spam, use it on sites you can control, so if you want to fill up a blog post or a forum post or get some transcriptions, do that. Set the time limit to 5 to 10 times the actual time, let's just make it 10 times. Just to make it simple for you, if you have a 5 minute job set the time limit to 50 minutes just because not everyone is as lightning fast as you and some people might have other things going on. Explain in step-by-step dummy-proof instructions so that they can't half-ass it, because we have all done that.

To save on headaches write out your instructions and then record a Camtasia video if you can just to make sure that they follow the instructions. exactly. Require them to post some kind of confirmation or their IP address on the reply box, because in the Turk itself they will have a place to reply.

So if you're doing forum or blog posts you can say "paste your response" or "paste what name you used to make the response" and then you can really quickly look at the site and make sure that it matches up.

Or you can say "Once you've done all this go to WhatIsMyIP.com, find your IP address and copy and paste it in this box". Then you can go and check your server logs or something and make sure that that person actually went and posted. Usually people will be honest, people aren't going to try to join a job and skip to the last step and try to confirm, most people are honest about this and the people who are going to try to cheat are going to be lazy and probably won't even give you that confirmation to begin with, so that's something to think about.

RobertPlankTraining.com

Chapter 6 - How Do You Pay For It?

You set up the project and you write the name and the description, so the name is what the job entails and the description will be - go to this URL, fill this out or do that.

Then you're going to specify the price per task which, if you're just testing the waters go from $0.05 to $0.25, so $0.25 would be a blog post, and $0.05 would be something like if you need to write something like "Rate my presentation 1 to 5 honestly". Don't say "Go here and click a 5", say "Honestly tell me what you as a human think about my video presentation, rate it 1 to 5".

Or you say "Reply to this blog post as a comment and I'll pay you $0.25" or "Reply to this forum post with a comment and I'll pay you $0.10". I would make the stuff on the $0.05 level stuff that takes you one click or takes you a few seconds so would be like drawing the sheep - drawing a sheep takes you a few seconds. Responding to a blog comment takes you about a minute or two. So if it takes a minute or two then $0.25; if it takes you a few seconds $0.05.

The amount of time allowed to perform the task, like I said, is 10 times the amount it would reasonably take you to perform the task because not everybody is as fast as you.

Then what? As people perform the tasks you can approve or deny the tasks and, I wish I didn't have to say this but I do - don't leave the page open and just keep refreshing and waiting and going in to approve every single task. Approve it once a day or twice a day, but never more than that. So just let the jobs pile up and after people complete it then you go in and approve them all at once, because otherwise it's going to be a huge time-suck, you're going to have to be switching back and forth between windows and I just wish I didn't have to say it, but so many people will let stuff like this take up all their time.

So as people perform the task you approve it or you deny it, and if you approve it then they get paid and the money goes into their Amazon account.

Chapter 7 - How Much Do You Charge Exactly?

If you're doing a blog post or a forum post or whatever, how much do you charge?

I would say $0.01 to $0.08 per minute of time you would expect it to take, depending on the skill.

For example with the sheep, you'd expect it to take maybe one minute, and that's really a low-level task so that's why he set it at 2 cents. But if you had someone replying to a blog post then you expect it to take maybe 2 or 3 minutes that's more high-level, that's more of a 6 or 7, so you would pay them maybe 25 cents.

I would just rate it 1 to 8, how much of a low-level or high-level task is this? Do they need to know English? That's more high level. Or do they just need to know how to move a mouse around a screen to draw a sheep? That's more low-level. Do they just need to watch a video and rate it 1 to 5? That's more low level, that's a 3 cent job.

So you decide on this spectrum, 1 to 8 cents, what's it worth? Then you price it on how long you would expect it to take? Then you just multiply that number value, the number of cents times the number of minutes it would take.

For example, if you have a blog post and you rate that as a 7 then you give them 7 cents a minute and you expect it to take 3 minutes. 7 times 3 is 21 so you'd give them about 21 cents per blog comment.

Never dedicate more than $50 to $100 for a project because you might screw up the description and forget about it for a couple of days. You go back and everyone has done the task but maybe you left out one little point. So maybe you said "I want you to give me a response on this blog post" and 50 people give you responses but you leave out the instructions on how to get the name and how to get the email address. So now you've given yourself a bunch of extra work to go and edit all those comments.

Or maybe they just left the comments out completely and it didn't allow them to submit it and they still want to be paid for their time.

You don't want to set a project for $500 and you wake up the next morning and you're out $500. So just dedicate $50 maximum starting out because you're going to want to tweak your projects. You're going to want to open a job with just a few slots and see how that works, then copy and paste the exact job and tweak it a little bit and see how that works until you've refined it, until you've got it systematized and then you can open it up to a ton of slots.

I'm not totally sure but if I was that guy, that artist doing the sheep thing, I would have tried it out on 20 people first, and if those 20 people had no problems with it I roll it out to a few more and a few more. Then once I was all done, I would go 'boom' 10,000 people please. Then that's when the easy work comes, that's when they just do all this stuff for you.

So never dedicate more than $50 to $100 for a project and at the beginning only

$30 maximum. Once you're used to doing these projects then do $100 maximum. You want to do that because you might screw something up and you don't want to waste a bunch of money # 1, and # 2, you're always going to want to tweak the instructions, so it's best to just have a few small projects.

Chapter 8 - Case Study

I was trying to help out one of my friends who was trying to get on a reality show for being a public speaker. But I didn't want to cheat the system – that was important, because I easily could have made a script or something that loaded the page a bunch of times and went through different proxies on different IP addresses and always rated him a 5. I wanted to earn it, I wanted to be honest.

He needed to get a set number of votes and then once he got the set number of votes he'd be in the top 10. Then out of those top 10 the people with the highest rating would get on to the show.

But at the time he only had 30 and he needed 300. So I mailed my list which I knew would get me about 100 or 200 votes but I needed that extra push.

So I created a $50 Turk job for some steady extra traffic. My instructions were: First of all get a name at FakeNameGenerator.com - depending on when you're watching this video, that site might be gone, there might be something better. So just Google for 'fake name generator' or some way to get a decent sounding name. Tell people to go there and get that name because you do not want people to use their own personal info, that's a big no no with the Turk, you can't tell people to put in their real name because Amazon doesn't want you to use it for building a list or for spamming or anything like that. So you want to tell people to get a fake name and go to this site, honestly rate this person from 1 to 5 and optionally leave a text comment so he can improve.

So we're saying we're doing something that a computer cannot do that a human has to do. A computer can go in and keep rating it a 5 but a computer can't look at the video and judge a person and rate them 1 to 5 and leave them a text comment.

So I said "Tell me if his delivery is good. Tell me if his content is good. Tell me if he is easy to understand. Tell me if the length of the video is good. Just leave a quick comment and rate from 1 to 5 so he can improve because we're testing this on humans".

I'm sure you're asking, how did that work?

Well using the job with the Turk and with my list we catapulted him from 30 votes to 300 votes in about a week, so we got him in the top ten, but we didn't cheat, we just got more eyeballs on the page, we got more traffic to that page and then it's up to the scoring system to decide how he ranked. To be honest I think using the Turk hurt his chances a little bit because before he was at a 9.5 out of 10 and then after, a lot of people in the Turk just didn't like his video and they bumped him down to 8.9, which is kind of funny, but the point is, we needed the votes to get him in that top ten so that he could at least be considered. Not only did we get the votes but we got lots of feedback and lots of ideas to improve his delivery.

But the point is that we were not cheating, we weren't using this for spamming or for building a list, we weren't using this to keep a rating of 5, we just wanted to get more people on the page to figure out where we were going wrong, to figure out how we could make it better and using humans in a way that you could not use computers.

Chapter 9 – Blog Comments

Here's another case study that's a little less blackhat.

I have a blog and you can call me vain or egotistical if you want but I like to have comments on my blog posts. So every time I make a blog post I hit my mailing list and I say "I just made this blog post, please go here and leave comments".

But I always try to take my list out of the equation. I wanted to make my list more of a selling list so I would keep pushing products on them with less free content, and every once in a while I get to the point when I am making so many blog posts then emailing my list 3 or 4 times a week just to alert them about new blog posts. I don't want to do that because that leaves very few chances to email them about paid stuff.

So I tried on one particular blog post, so don't think that I fill up my blog comments with lots of fake comments, ok. These are all from most of the people on my list but for one single blog entry I wanted to see if I could outsource the blog commenting to people other than those who are on my list, just random strangers.

So I made a job in the Turk and I said: Go to my URL here and read my blog post. And the blog post ends in a question so I want you to leave a comment using a fake first name from the fake name generator and set the email address as noreply@example.com so that I know that it's one of you guys, because I don't want to confuse you guys with the real people who are trying to get on a list and trying to get more information, I'm just using you to add more content – I'm outsourcing the content creation.

I said: Type a thoughtful comment with your best trick on whatever the subject was - so I would teach a few hints and I would ask a question and I would say “give me your best trick” and leave it up to them to figure out how they would answer that. They could go to Google and do a little bit of searching, they could go to forums, they could ask friends, they could just use common sense or their personal knowledge and it was a really simple question like ‘how do you improve offers?’ or something. They could use examples from commercials or television or from websites – they just used their knowledge as a layperson to answer the question.

For my guidelines I said to make it at least three sentences long because I didn’t want people to give me a bunch of one-word answers and expect to get paid, even though I think it was only about $0.25. Then I said "Post a copy of your response in the feedback so that I can match it up to a real person and approve it", and I read all my blog comments so that if I read all the posts in the feedback for the Turk job I would pretty easily recognize if something was out of place and if everything looked good I would just select everything and approve them all.

The result was that I gave them $0.25 of payment and gave them 20 minutes to complete the job. I was just doing this as a small test and I was impatient so I didn't let it run for longer than 12 hours, I just set it up at night before I went to bed. I went to sleep, came back and I had 7 blog comments in 8 hours and the total cost was $1.75 plus a couple more cents in fees. That's pretty cool right, $1.75 to get 7 blog comments. If you went to a freelancer, you'd have to pay 10 or 20 bucks for 7 blog comments, and most of them were pretty good, they weren't great, they weren't from experts but they were a lot better than I had expected. I had expected 4th or 5th grade term paper type of stuff, really dumb responses but people actually had some pretty good answers.

I told a couple of people this story at a seminar once and then said "I dare you to go to my blog and figure out which of these comments are left by real people and which of these were outsourced" and they couldn't tell. I could tell just because the quality was 10 percent less but it was really tough to tell.

Chapter 10 – Other Uses For Mechanical Turk?

Here are some other ways you could use Mechnical Turk for Crowdsourcing.

You could do forum posts, you could do blog posts, what are the other uses?

You could create a **survey**. You could make a survey asking the question: how many hours of television do you watch during the day? Maybe you wanted to use that as a statistic on your sales letter. You could go and find the old boring statistics but you wanted to find out right now how much people watched on television.

So you say "Here's my survey" and you have the different radio buttons, you just use some simple survey script and you say:

- Do you watch 2 hours or less of television a day?
- Do you watch 2 to 3 hours?
- Do you watch 4 to 6 hours?
- Or do you watch more than 7 hours a day?"

Then they just choose one, they click submit and you show their IP address or a confirmation number that they can paste into the feedback form, or you can say "Paste in the feedback form what your response was - did you respond 2 to 4 hours, did you respond 7+ hours, just paste the response in".

That's a really low tech way to get people to respond to surveys, you have them use the URL just so that you can easily total up the results, you don't have to worry about cutting and pasting a bunch of stuff. But then you have them paste their answer in the feedback form and something that simple (people aren't going to be going to the survey and copying their choice and pasting in the feedback without clicking the radio button) they're going to answer the survey usually.

You could poll that to ten thousand people at 2 cents each then you can say "I went out and asked ten thousand people how much TV they watched and 60% said they watch more than 7 hours - and this isn't just some statistic – I actually asked all these ten thousand people and they said they watch more than 7 hours, so here is my 14 page report on how to get your child to watch less TV during the week".

So a simple way to use the Turk is for survey purposes to use as proof.

You could get people to help you name a product. So you could say - here is my product on this and this and this, here are the possible keywords I could use in the domain name, please go to this URL where you can do domain whois's and find a good .com domain name that includes one, two or three of these keywords. Or you could just say – what do you think of when I describe this? Or you can make it a survey so you say – I'm torn between these three names, I'm torn between TV Watching Killer or Get Your Child to Stop Watching TV or Get Your Child to Watch Half the TV He or She Watches Now in Less Than 6 Minutes Guaranteed! And you make it a three option survey and you send people to that URL and say “Can you just click on this thing and submit it so that I get the answer and then respond in the feedback box what your submission was”.

You could just watch people who come to your site - so you could use it to get quick traffic to your site and you could say “All you need to do is stay on this site for at least 5 minutes and read the sales letter or click around on stuff, but just stay on there for 5 minutes, and paste your IP address in the feedback box so that I can confirm that you were on my page for 5 minutes”. You can use that to find the sticking point in your sales letters - you can use a service like ClickTale where you can actually see what people see on their computer screens when they visit your site, so you can say – they were at this part, then they scrolled down, they scrolled back up, then they read this – so you can see where the sticking points are. You can see if someone was reading and at some point they just stopped or they closed the window and you can say "Hmm, that headline kind of sucks, maybe I can change it to something else to see if it gets people to keep reading".

Or you could use software so if you have a script online and you have a demo version which people can login and mess around with you can say "Alright go here and enter 'demo' as the username, 'demo' as the password and click around and try and get it to work and then perform this task". Then you can say "Even if you can't get the task done I'll still pay you but do your best to try to finish it", so you'll be able to see how intuitive your interface is.

You could use it to split test a website so you have a site and you have Version A and Version B of a site, and site A is laid out a certain way and site B is laid out a certain way; you can send all the traffic here and say "Post in the feedback form if you were Version A or Version B and were you able to get to such and such page" and you have a list of links over here and some links over there and some drop down boxes here and you try to figure out if your software or your script is easy enough that if you give somebody a task they can navigate the menus and they can click on something and do something and get the final result.

I understand this might not apply to you but if you do any kind of programming or any kind of software development this is very valuable because, in many serious software companies especially those in large cities, they'll pull people off the street and record them with a camera and ask them to try to do something with a piece of software then they will figure out what they try to do and record if they get the task done or not.

So you can almost get inside people's heads and figure out what they are thinking and doing when they read your sales letter, what they are thinking and doing when they try out your software, what they are thinking and doing when they try out your membership site. So if you use a service like ClickTale which documents what they do you can get a lot of good data this way.

Chapter 11 – Cool Story

Here is one final cool story before we go. Crowdsourcing was used a few years ago to try to find this man Steve Fossett, he was a pilot and he was famous for a lot of things, mainly in 2005 he performed the first solo non stop unrefueled circumnavigation of the world, so he flew round the entire world in a plane by himself without stopping and without getting a refuel.

But in September 2007 he was going from I think Nevada to California, not sure about that, but he took a trip on his plane, he didn't leave a flight plan and he flew over the Nevada Desert and the plane went missing. People were trying to find the wreckage so Google retrieved current satellite imagery of the Nevada Desert and then a few days later fifty thousand people joined the search (they had put all these images online) and fifty thousand people inspected thirty thousand satellite images to try to find clues of where the plane landed because that's a lot of desert to look through. Even if you sent out search parties and people looked at satellite photos themselves there was just so much stuff to look at.

The result was they didn't find him and people attribute that to the layperson not really knowing what kind of stuff to look for when they are looking for wreckage, but the point is fifty thousand people helped, fifty thousand people did a little tiny bit of work and it added up to hundreds and thousands of man hours of work otherwise for free. So that's just something to consider.

RobertPlankTraining.com

Chapter 12 – Common Sense with the Turk System

Don't get carried away - start small then refine your business system. Limit your jobs to $50 maximum. Limit your jobs to 20 or 30 people at first and then build it up and up and up.

Don't expect the world - there are a lot of factors, a lot of places where it could go wrong. You might word the thing differently, you might have some stupid idea or you might just plain screw up. So don't expect the world because this is general unskilled labor. My best advice to you is to look at other jobs, other Human Intelligent Tasks that are on the Turk and duplicate them or adjust them to fit your needs, to fit your website.

Chapter 13 – Summary

Here's what we talked about in this book for using the Mechanical Turk successfully.

- First of all use the one to eight cent per minute rate, so figure out if the thing they are doing is more on the one cent side or the eight cent side. If something is in the middle maybe its worth four cents, if it's more involved, it takes more skill maybe, it's more on the eight cents side.

- Then multiply the amount you are going to pay per minute times the number of minutes it takes to do that.
- Even if you chose eight cents a minute remember that's only about five dollars, so that is not even minimum wage but you also have to consider that many people will get the job done more quickly than you assign it as, and they might be doing something else so it's not like their time is totally devoted to that full hour you give them.
- Allot five to ten times the time it should take so if you are having them leave a blog comment and it

takes three minutes, give them fifteen or even thirty minutes to just leave a simple blog comment, because some people are slow.

- Never ever ask them to click ads or for example always click 5 when rating a video.
- Never ask for personal information - so ask them to provide a fake name.
- Ask for an honest opinion and ask for research.

Chapter 14 – Conclusion

The Turk is not just a way for clever artists to monetize their sheep drawing website, you can use this to fill up blog comments, you can use this to populate forums, you can use this to get feedback on your video, you can use this to transcribe your videos or your audios and you can use it for user-testing on your sales letters and on your scripts.

I would like to thank you for taking the time to learn all about how to properly use the Amazon Mechanical Turk to crowd source your next freelancing job to get a lot of people to do simple tasks for pennies instead of getting one person who might be unreliable to do a single task for a lot more money.

Robert Plank
RobertPlankTraining.com

www.ingramcontent.com/pod-product-compliance
Lightning Source LLC
Chambersburg PA
CBHW022105170526
45157CB00004B/1494

9781461112136